Let Not Your Heart Be Troubled

Jason Curry

ISBN 978-1-68517-178-0 (paperback)
ISBN 978-1-68517-179-7 (digital)

Christian Faith Publishing
832 Park Avenue
Meadville, PA 16335
www.christianfaithpublishing.com

Printed in the United States of America

Foreword

I began working on this devotional after being laid off after ten years with the company. During the past few months since being laid off, I reflected on all the ways God has tested my faith and allowed things to happen that were sometimes very tough to go through. I did not always handle the circumstances, some brought on by myself, very well. Through it all I have found God to be true to His word and never has let me go. The stories and experiences from my forty-one-year walk with Christ, and the lessons I've learned will, I hope, encourage you, perhaps convict you, but ultimately strengthen your relationship with our Heavenly Father and make it richer.

Bedtime Prayer

Now I lay me down to sleep
I know my soul the Lord will keep
If I die whilst I sleep
I'll awake to sit at my Savior's feet
I'll see all those who've gone before
Father, Grandfather, on that bright shore
I'll sit and watch and wait for you
Then welcome you home with quite a view
To spend the years as they roll by
In happiness forever in the sweet by and by

Lord, Where Are You?

Part One

I have long since lost count how many times I have spoken these words out loud in my mind, in my prayers…words that, if a follower of Christ is honest, has spoken throughout their lives for one reason or another. The circumstances can be varied as the reasons can be.

One I would like to zero in on is, I confess, when I feel God has left or drawn himself away because of my own shortcomings or disobedience. Why do Christians feel this way? Doesn't God's Word say he will never leave us or forsake us? Doesn't God's Word say there is nothing that can separate us from his love? Yes, on both counts. But why then do we feel this way? That is a difficult answer to put into just a few sentences.

I remember a dear preacher, James Webber, who was one of the elders in Faith Baptist Church where I attended for many years say more than once, "If you don't feel close to God, guess who moved?" God will be as close to us as we desire him to be. We move away from God, never the other way around.

The parable of the prodigal son is a perfect example. A child leaves his father and pursues their own desires in the world. The father watched and waited for the son to return. And when the son finally did, he ran to him to welcome him home. There was no "I told you so" moment and no judgement. Just complete, unconditional, and overwhelming love, forgiveness, restoration, and celebration. And this will always be the case. I know. Your circumstances, no matter what they are or how they happened, can never be more powerful than God's love for you.

> Draw nigh to God, and he will draw nigh to you. (James 4:8 KJV)

> …I have loved thee with an everlasting love. (Jeremiah 31:3 KJV)

Thoughts and Notes:

_____
_____
_____
_____
_____
_____
_____
_____
_____
_____
_____
_____

Today's' Prayer

Father, thank you for never casting me aside when I sin against you and leave you for my own selfish desires. Help me to never be afraid to come back to you because you will always be waiting for me with open arms. Amen.

DAY TWO

Lord, Where Are You?

Part Two

The world's problems and trials can become so overwhelming they can keep us from feeling God's presence if we allow them to, sometimes without us realizing it. We focus on the problem instead of the problem solver. We hop on the internet to find the latest solution for our problems instead of taking them to the one who created us and is intimately aware of our weaknesses and trials we go through. You are never alone despite feeling that way. How we feel is not necessarily the best way to judge ourselves. Grab hold of God with a death grip and do not let go until you feel close to him again. What helped me on so many occasions when I was struggling with something was listening to hymns and music. The words to so many of the greatest, such as "It Is Well with My Soul," were born out of circumstances from intense sadness, loneliness, and suffering. Music can speak to us in unique and profound ways.

"His Eye Is on the Sparrow" (Civilla D. Martin, 1905)

Why should I feel discouraged,
Why should the shadows come,
Why should my heart be lonely,
And long for heav'n and home;
When Jesus is my portion?
My constant Friend is He;
His eye is on the sparrow,
And I know He watches me;

"Let not your heart be troubled,"
His tender word I hear,
And resting on His goodness,
I lose my doubts and fears;
Though by the path he leadeth,
But one step I may see;
His eye is on the sparrow,
And I know he watches me;

Whenever I am tempted,
Whenever clouds arise;
When songs give place to sighing,
When hope within me dies,
I draw the closer to him,
From care he sets me free;
His eye is on the sparrow,
And I know he watches me;

Thoughts and Notes:

_____

_____

_____

_____

_____

_____

_____

_____

_____

_____

_____

_____

Today's Prayer

Jesus, thank you for always keeping your eyes on me. Please help me to always remember to listen to what your word says and not my feelings. Thank you for your promises and help me to never doubt them. Amen.

The Blueprint

In this old hymn, there is a blueprint of how we should deal with trials. Jesus bears our burdens. We should take every burden and grief to him and never try to carry them alone. Jesus knows where we are weakest. He will never leave or forsake us. All burdens, not some, will he carry.

Every care, grief, temptation, and sorrow should be taken to Jesus.

"What a Friend We Have in Jesus"
(Joseph Scriven, 1855)

What a friend we have in Jesus,
all our sins and griefs to bear!
What a privilege to carry
everything to God in prayer!
O what peace we often forfeit,
O what needless pain we bear,
all because we do not carry
everything to God in prayer!

Have we trials and temptations?
Is there trouble anywhere?
We should never be discouraged;
take it to the Lord in prayer!
Can we find a friend so faithful?
who will all our sorrows share?

Jesus knows our every weakness;
take it to the Lord in prayer!

Are we weak and heavy laden,
cumbered with a load of care?
Precious Savior, still our refuge—
take it to the Lord in prayer!
Do your friends despise, forsake you?
Take it to the Lord in prayer!
In his arms he'll take and shield you;
you will find a solace there.

Thoughts and Notes:

_____
_____
_____
_____
_____
_____
_____
_____
_____
_____
_____
_____
_____

Today's Prayer

Dear Jesus, thank you for being my Savior. Help me to live the words of this song and to always come to you with every care and every burden. Remind me daily of the strength and grace I will find when I come to you. Amen.

Lord, I'm So Tired and Weary

Life can throw some really crazy curveballs at us that come literally out of nowhere. I certainly wasn't expecting to trip and fall and severely injure my shoulder in November of 2018. I went through a surgery and months of painful physical therapy twice within two years. Even though the second surgery went well, and I have full use of my right shoulder now, there was so much damage from the injury that every day it is going to hurt to some degree. I face eventual shoulder replacement surgery down the road.

I would love to be able to pick up and play my trombone again and regain the skill level I once had, but as yet, I am unable to for very long at all due to the soreness I get in my shoulder. I wake up daily to a very stiff and sore back. Many times it doesn't matter how or where I sit the throbbing and constant pain is there and definitely something I wish I didn't have. I would be lying to say some days it doesn't affect my attitude and motivation. But I always find strength and grace by going to Jesus and telling him exactly what I am feeling and how much my back hurts or my shoulder. He already knows this, but telling him and admitting I cannot make it on my own does amazing things. Whatever struggle you are going through, in whatever form it takes, can be endured if you but lean on him.

Talk with Jesus as you would a close friend. There _is_ grace in abundance at the Savior's feet. Do not doubt. He is faithful. Jesus knows what it is like to be tired. He was completely human and experienced sorrow, grief, and all the frailties we do. We are his children and he loves us dearly. Let your Savior know how hard it may be for you. Rest in his love and grace.

I life up my eyes to the mountains—where does my help come from? My help comes from the LORD, the Maker of heaven and earth. (Psalm 121:1–2 NIV)

Thoughts and Notes:

_____
_____
_____
_____
_____
_____
_____
_____
_____
_____
_____
_____

Today's Prayer

Lord, let me draw strength from you when I face pain and sorrow. You are the perfect place to find sojourn when I need rest and relief. Help me to confess to you when I am hurting and I don't understand, believing you will reach down and pick me up in your arms and hold me. Amen.

Take my yoke upon you, and learn of me;
for I am meek and lowly in heart: and ye shall
find rest unto your souls. (Matthew 11:29 KJV)

The King Is Coming

Jesus is coming soon! How often do we stop and dwell on this? I mean really stop and think about this? I think many have adopted a rather nonchalant attitude about the second coming of Christ. I will not discuss the different eschatological views here about timing, and will the church go through the tribulation, etc. He is coming though. Whether six months or six years from now knowing he is coming and what that will mean for you can lift you out of a period of depression, anxiety, or trials.

For me no more daily back pain, shoulder pain, and neck pain. No waking up and taking several minutes to get up out of bed. No more psoriasis all over my body. These things alone would be amazing. You will never again be tired or sleepy or know what pain is. No more cancer, no more diseases…get the picture? Focus on that moment when you will finally see his face and know that you are going home. Think of the reunion you will have with loved ones who have gone before you. Dwell on the moment the *King is coming* and we shall behold him face-to-face.

> But as it is written, Eye hath not seen, nor ear heard, neither have entered into the heart of man, the things which God hath prepared for them that love him. (1 Corinthians 2:9 KJV)

> And God shall wipe away all tears from their eyes; and there shall be no more death, neither sorrow, nor crying, neither shall there be any

more pain: for the former things are passed away. (Revelation 21:4 KJV)

Thoughts and Notes:

_____

_____

_____

_____

_____

_____

_____

_____

_____

_____

_____

_____

_____

Today's Prayer

Dear Jesus, please help me keep looking forward to your return. Help me to rejoice now in what will happen one day when I see you face-to-face. Help me to focus on that moment when I feel depressed and sad about what is going on in my life and in the world. In your precious name, Amen.

Be of Good Cheer

These things I have spoken unto you, that in me ye might have peace. In the world ye shall have tribulation: but be of good cheer; I have overcome the world. (John 16:33 KJV)

Jesus spoke these words to his disciples just before he would be taken away to be crucified. He was preparing them for his departure back to the Father. He was telling them in advance they would suffer tribulation but also gave them a promise of peace. He did not say he may overcome or will eventually overcome the world but that he had already overcome the world. Nothing the world throws at us can defeat us. We have overcome the world through Christ. Remember this promise when you think you cannot go on. Whatever you are going through claim victory over it through Christ. When faced with something that seems to be overwhelming, I have found that thanking God for it and thanking him for everything he does every day for us can help me refocus my mind and heart. We are not just conquerors but more than conquerors.

Nay, in all these things we are more than conquerors through him that loved us. (Romans 8:37 KJV)

Thoughts and Notes:

Today's Prayer

Lord, please help me to understand that tribulation and trials are a part of my walk with you and that you will always be by my side and, if necessary, carry me through each and every one of them. You conquered and overcame the world so help me be a conqueror through you. Amen.

Yet Not I

> I am crucified with Christ: nevertheless I live; yet not I, but Christ liveth in me: and the life which I now live in the flesh I live by the faith of the Son of God, who loved me, and gave himself for me. (Galatians 2:20 KJV)

This verse explains that our sin, our guilt, and our penalty for that sin and guilt was dealt with on the cross. Past, present, and future. We also became victors over the world and all that it tries to throw at us. We should endeavor to face each trial and problem we face from a position of victory, leaning completely on Christ, who has already overcome the world. Many times in my life after trying and failing to stand on my own and handling a tough situation I had to swallow my pride and stubborn will and stand in the strength that God will give freely and abundantly. He helped me finally overcome the anger I felt toward the church I attended in my youth because I felt they were not there for me after my dad died from cancer when I was fifteen.

Christ is the solid rock: stand in his strength and you will not be shaken. Go to the scriptures and read. Start with the Psalms if you are not sure what to read.

> My hope is built on nothing less
> than Jesus' blood and righteousness.
> I dare not trust the sweetest frame
> but wholly lean on Jesus' name.

In ev'ry rough and stormy gale,
my anchor holds within the vale.
When all around my soul gives way,
he then is all my hope and stay.

"The Solid Rock" (Edward Mote, 1834)

Thoughts and Notes:

_____
_____
_____
_____
_____
_____
_____
_____
_____
_____
_____
_____

Today's Prayer

Father, I thank you that I did not have to pay the penalty for my sin. I can rest in the promise that it was paid for by you when you died on the cross for me. Let me always remember that this world and all its wiles have no power over me because I have conquered the world through you. Let me stand in your strength, my solid rock. Amen.

...If God be for us, who can be against us?
(Romans 8:31 KJV)

Forgive Yourself

Let's be honest. Our own choices and decisions can sometimes be the source of our troubles and trials. I blew it big-time when I first went to college because I did not focus and I didn't know why I was there (which was to study and learn). My grades fell, and I lost qualifications for student aid to continue. I was definitely not ready for college when I left. I lacked the discipline to balance studies properly. Although I continued playing and singing for years after I eventually stopped for a very long time and often I used that failure to tell myself it was not worth pursuing anymore.

What I want to emphasize is this. Life is not over, and you are not a failure just because you didn't do something right. You may have failed at a task or relationship, but this does not mean you are a failure. Do not spend wasted time beating yourself up over and over again for something that you did or was done to you. Forgive yourself and forgive whomever did something to you if that is the case.

When you do make mistakes, acknowledge it and ask forgiveness if it affected someone else. But do not let it cause you to think that you have lost value, especially in the sight of God. The Bible is full of people who really blew it. Some worse than I wager you ever will, and yet they were still loved and even blessed by God. David conspired to have a man murdered because he wanted to cover up his adultery with Bathsheba, and he was called a man after God's own heart. Do not let past actions cause you to think for a minute you cannot be used by God and are not worthy of his mercy and grace. We never were worthy; that is the whole point of his mercy and grace.

Thoughts and Notes:

_____
_____
_____
_____
_____
_____
_____
_____
_____
_____
_____
_____
_____
_____

Today's Prayer

My Lord and Savior, please help me to let go of all the guilt and shame I feel for my past mistakes. Help me to see myself through your eyes and accept your forgiveness and help me to forgive myself. Help me always to remember I am always in your care no matter what I do or have done. In your name. Amen.

Nothing Between

I would like to share this old song by Charles Tindley in 1905. This should be every child of God's goal. Not easy to accomplish but through Christ it can be done.

Verse 1: Nothing between my soul and the Savior, Naught of this world's delusive dream; I have renounced all sinful pleasure, Jesus is mine, there's nothing between.

Verse 2: Nothing between like worldly pleasure; Habits of life, tho' harmless they seem; Must not my heart from Him ever sever, He is my all, there's nothing between.

Verse 3: Nothing between like pride or station; Self or friends shall not intervene; Tho' it may cost me much tribulation, I am resolved, there's nothing between.

Verse 4: Nothing between e'en many hard trials, Tho' the whole world against me convene;

Watching with pray'r and much self-denial, I'll triumph at last, there's nothing between.

Is there a habit you have that seems to be innocent that is taking time away from God's Word? Is your job, a friend, or a relationship hindering your walk with Him? If so, then perhaps it is time to carefully examine things or persons in your life and ask one question: Does this person, activity, or job help or hinder my walk with Christ?

Putting aside everything that hinders your walk can be a very hard thing to do. I still fail in this regard sometimes. It is a daily battle we must fight. One we cannot effectively do alone, but it is a battle that we can win for Jesus has already won it for us. Through Jesus, we can shape our lives so there will be nothing between you and your savior.

Thoughts and Notes:

_____

_____

_____

_____

_____

_____

_____

_____

_____

_____

_____

_____

_____

Today's Prayer

Heavenly Father, please help me examine my life and habits to see if anything is preventing my complete fellowship with you. Help me to put you first in every aspect of my life so there is nothing between us. In Jesus's name. Amen.

DAY 10

Pray and Praise

There are things I wish I knew the answer to when it comes to reading the Bible. I am sure I am not alone here. It would be interesting to know, given my love for music, what hymn Jesus and his disciples sang after their last supper. And it would be interesting to know what Paul and Silas sang when they were in prison and their jail cells busted open when they began to pray and sing. I heard it said once the reason there was an earthquake was because God was tapping his foot to the music. That isn't in the Bible, but it'll preach, right?

Jail cells during that time were nothing like the air-conditioned ones with beds, meals, sanitation, etc. we have today. They were not places you ever wanted to end up. They were usually a hole in the ground with no sanitation and the critters to keep you company. And food? Maybe if you were lucky. Yet Paul and Silas did two things current day Christians do not always do when faced with trials and tribulation. They prayed and sang from a place you would not think anyone would even think about doing. We will just give up entirely and think there is no way out.

What type of prison are you in today? Physical? Mental? Both? Whatever fashion it takes, try to follow Paul and Silas' example even though you may not feel like it. Will the prison cell burst open and your chains fall off? Try it and see. I know from experience it will definitely make dealing with it so much easier.

Thoughts and Notes:

_____

_____

_____

_____

_____

_____

_____

_____

_____

_____

_____

_____

_____

Today's Prayer

Jesus, help me, as your servants Paul and Silas did, to have a heart of prayer and praise in the most difficult times of my life. Let my voice lift itself in praise to you despite my circumstances and let your peace, joy, and power flow through my praise. In your precious name. Amen.

You Are Precious and Valuable

> I will praise thee; for I am fearfully and wonderfully made: marvelous are thy works; and that my soul knoweth right well. My substance was not hid from thee, when I was made in secret, and curiously wrought in the lowest parts of the earth. Thine eyes did see my substance, yet being unperfect; and in thy book all my members were written, which in continuance were fashioned, when as yet there was none of them. How precious also are thy thoughts unto me, O God! how great is the sum of them! If I should count them, they are more in number than the sand: when I awake, I am still with thee. (Psalm 139:14–18 KJV)

There is a misused phrase often told to children: "Sticks and stones may break my bones, but names will never hurt me." How incredibly wrong that is. Whether it is making fun of how someone looks, making fun of their name, or because of a disability, the deepest hurts and feelings of worthlessness come from people who say harsh words and who make fun of and put us down. This isn't restricted to our childhood years either. The effects of this can be devastating.

For the child of God, our self-worth must come first from our heavenly father. The Bible tells us in so many places how much we mean to God. When we get away from spending time in his word and in prayer, the world around us can easily manipulate us into thinking poorly of ourselves. A favorite tactic of the enemy is to make us feel like we have lost our relationship with God and to ridicule us, especially for things done in our past.

We are also bombarded with advertisements saying get this or that and you'll be better and be happier. Being adults doesn't mean they are immune to these types of feelings. This is also why it is essential for each person to be part of a God-fearing, Bible-believing church that preaches the truth so we will find that group of people who can uplift and encourage us.

Thoughts and Notes:

_____

_____

_____

_____

_____

_____

_____

_____

_____

_____

_____

_____

Today's Prayer

Father, please help me to love myself as you do. I thank and praise you that never stop watching over me. Help me to drown myself in your word and help me to maintain my focus on you and not the world. Help me to ignore what the world may tell me about myself and only look to you for my self-worth. Amen.

Stay Strong

We are troubled on every side, yet not distressed; we are perplexed, but not in despair; Persecuted, but not forsaken; cast down, but not destroyed; Always bearing about in the body the dying of the Lord Jesus, that the life also of Jesus might be made manifest in our body. (2 Corinthians 4:8–10 KJV)

For all things are for your sakes, that the abundant grace might through the thanksgiving of many redound to the glory of God. For which cause we faint not; but though our outward man perish, yet the inward man is renewed day by day. For our light affliction, which is but for a moment, worketh for us a far more exceeding and eternal weight of glory; While we look not at the things which are seen, but at the things which are not seen: for the things which are seen are temporal; but the things which are not seen are eternal. (2 Corinthians 4:15–18 KJV)

No matter what you go through keep your focus on Christ. Whatever it may be is only temporary. Paul knew what tribulation felt like. He spent many years in various prisons and experienced a direct and long-term attack from Satan in his thorn in the flesh. He encourages the Corinthians not to lose sight of the end goal. Our problems, trials, and persecutions are only temporary, and God has promised his children they can never defeat us when we trust him and lean on him. I have long since lost count how many times during the years after my father died where I had serious doubts if I could go on. But I am still here, stronger, wiser, and firmly believing that if I trust God to supply whatever strength I may require, I will make it and so will you. Believe.

Thoughts and Notes:

_____
_____
_____
_____
_____
_____
_____
_____
_____
_____
_____
_____
_____

Today's Prayer

Dear Jesus, help me to have the right attitude when I am faced with tribulations. Help me to remember that they are only temporary and that you sometimes allow these things to help me grow and become more like you. Give me the grace to endure and help me to draw all my strength from you. Amen.

Day 13

Count It All Joy

> My brethren, count it all joy when ye fall into divers temptations; Knowing this, that the trying of your faith worketh patience. (James 1:2–3 KJV)

So something negative comes into your life or you fall into an intense struggle against a temptation. Let me guess the first thing you want to do is be joyous, right? Let's take a short look into the life of Fanny Crosby, a pioneer in the world of hymn writing and poems in the nineteenth and early twentieth centuries. When she was three weeks of age, she lost her eyesight after mustard poultice was put on her eyes to treat inflammation from a cold. She said of her accident, "It seemed intended by the blessed providence of God that I should be blind all my life, and I thank him for the dispensation. If perfect earthly sight were [*sic*] offered me tomorrow I would not accept it. I might not have sung hymns to the praise of God if I had been distracted by the beautiful and interesting things about me."[1]

She led a truly remarkable life. Imagine what it was like when she went to be with her Lord and the first face she saw was that of her Savior. Certainly we will not all be Fanny Crosby, but her disability lasted her entire life, yet she was used mightily by God. Your trial or temptation is part of a journey that all Christians take and go

---

[1] Fanny Crosby, *America's Hymn Queen*, Christianity.com, 2010, http://www.christianhistorytimeline.com/GLIMPSEF/Glimpses2/glimpses198.shtml.

through. No matter what it is, God is still sovereign and in complete control. Know that his purpose for you is always for your good. Your trial is not too severe or temptation too strong that God will not sustain you through it. Even a disability. Surrender yourself to the potter and let Christ mold you into something wonderful and beautiful.

Thoughts and Notes:

_____

_____

_____

_____

_____

_____

_____

_____

_____

_____

_____

_____

_____

Today's Prayer

Dear Jesus, please help me think of what I can do through your strength and not what I cannot do when I am faced with what I see as an insurmountable obstacle. Let me have the right perspective and not fall into despair, knowing that you can accomplish your purpose in me no matter what may happen. Amen.

Yea, though I walk through the valley of the
shadow of death, _I will fear no evil: for thou art
with me;_ thy rod and thy staff they comfort me.
(Psalm 23:4 KJV)

How's Your Faith?

The greatest miracle, save perhaps his birth, was the resurrection of Christ. It is not just some religious theory or something that cannot be proved. Great effort has been made trying to disprove this and yet no one has succeeded. There is an abundance of historical proof that Jesus was first completely and thoroughly dead by crucifixion, and that he was seen afterward completely alive.

This cannot be said of any other so-called religious leader of any religion. Jesus conquered death so we have nothing to fear from it. And if death, the great enemy of our souls, is powerless over us, what then should we ever be afraid of? Why do we sell ourselves short and think we may never defeat temptation or addiction? Why is our faith so weak? The same Holy Spirit that raised Jesus from the dead is in us. Do we not see miracles or great victories in our life because we do not ask or do we just not believe?

Jesus explained to the disciples when they asked why they couldn't cast a demon out of a lad and what the issue was.

> And Jesus said unto them, Because of your unbelief: for verily I say unto you, If ye have faith as a grain of mustard seed, ye shall say unto this mountain, Remove hence to yonder place; and it shall remove; and nothing shall be impossible unto you. (Matthew 17:20 KJV)

Our lack of or weakness of our belief is the result of a weak faith.

Strengthen your faith by immersing yourself in God's Word daily and in prayer. Not just a few minutes here or there. Set aside an hour or more to spend time in prayer. It will make a huge difference in your life. You will discover that when a test of your faith comes along, you can face it with unwavering trust in God.

Thoughts and Notes:

_____

_____

_____

_____

_____

_____

_____

_____

_____

_____

_____

_____

_____

Today's Prayer

Jesus, help me grow to have unshakable faith in you. Help me to believe all things are possible because you have conquered sin, death, and the world. Speak to me through your word and help me to have faith like Abraham did. Amen.

Truly my soul waiteth upon God: from him
cometh my salvation. He only is my rock and my
salvation; he is my defense; I shall not be greatly
moved. (Psalm 62:1–2 KJV)

Victorious Confession

Have mercy upon me, O God, according to thy lovingkindness: according unto the multitude of thy tender mercies blot out my transgressions. Wash me throughly from mine iniquity, and cleanse me from my sin. For I acknowledge my transgressions: and my sin is ever before me. Against thee, thee only, have I sinned, and done this evil in thy sight: that thou mightest be justified when thou speakest, and be clear when thou judgest. Behold, I was shapen in iniquity; and in sin did my mother conceive me. Behold, thou desirest truth in the inward parts: and in the hidden part thou shalt make me to know wisdom. Purge me with hyssop, and I shall be clean: wash me, and I shall be whiter than snow. Make me to hear joy and gladness; that the bones which thou hast broken may rejoice. Hide thy face from my sins, and blot out all mine iniquities. Create in me a clean heart, O God; and renew a right spirit within me. Cast me not away from thy presence; and take not thy holy spirit from me. Restore unto me the joy of thy salvation; and uphold me with thy free spirit. (Psalm 51:1–12 KJV)

Here we see David's repentant prayer after being confronted by the prophet, Nathan, for his transgression with Bathsheba and the murder of her husband. This was one of David's lowest points. God forgave him to be sure, but he had to live with the fallout. While we, as imperfect, fallen beings, may really blow it and have to live with the consequences. Our walk and relationship with our heavenly Father can grow stronger and richer in spite of it.

I have, in error, sometimes thought I had to fight the battle and had to deal with the consequences of a poor choice alone but that is the furthest thing from the truth. We must face all of life from a standing of victory because we have already overcome the world through Christ. I will say this again and again: spend time alone with Jesus every day, we were not meant to face life alone so why do it?

Are you at a point in your life where you've done something similar to what David did? Cry out to God and seek his forgiveness.

Thoughts and Notes:

_____

_____

_____

_____

_____

_____

_____

_____

_____

_____

_____

_____

Today's Prayer

Dear merciful Father, forgive me when I have really blown it. Renew my relationship with you and restore my joy. Give me grace to deal with whatever consequences may come and let me know the peace that you promise. Amen.

If we confess our sins, he is faithful and just to forgive us our sins, and to cleanse us from all unrighteousness. (1 John 1:9 KJV)

Never Late

Have you been praying about a certain issue, problem, or person in your life but nothing seems to be happening? Do you spend hours in prayer over weeks and months or longer but there has been no change?

Let us turn to the eleventh chapter of John. Here we see the story of Jesus and the raising of Lazarus. Jesus was only a short distance away when he was told Lazarus was sick. So he could have been there within a very short time but he waited, and it was four days after Lazarus died before he arrived at Bethany where Lazarus was buried. Both Martha and Mary said if only Jesus were here Lazarus would not have died. Jesus's response to Martha was to ask if she believed he was the resurrection and the life. She did believe, but her focus was far into the future. Jesus was met by a weeping Mary and he himself was so moved that he, too, wept because he groaned in the spirit. How much does Jesus love his children! Imagine Martha and Mary's reaction after. Did they think he was there to resurrect Lazarus? It didn't seem like it.

Do you believe that his timing is perfect? Waiting on his timing can be one of the most difficult things a Christian can do. It can shake our faith and cause doubt to infiltrate our thoughts and beliefs. Jesus is not unaware of our limitations and knows how difficult it is for us to wait for his timing. When we try to force things it ends badly. There is a song, "Four Days Late," that I often listen to as a reminder that when God does show up in his time, something incredible happens that is so much better than we were hoping for. Dear child of God, rest assured that God is already in the future working everything out. Trust in his timing.

Thoughts and Notes:

_____

_____

_____

_____

_____

_____

_____

_____

_____

_____

_____

_____

_____

Today's Prayer

Lord, teach me patience when I am waiting for your timing. Help me to understand that you are already in the future working out things for my good and that the blessing you have in mind is much greater than I think. Help me to trust in your way. Amen.

Give Everything

Casting all your care upon him; for he
careth for you. (1 Peter 5:7 KJV)

The verse is very specific here. Casting *all*, not just some of your anxieties. How our human pride likes to hold on to a piece of our sorrow or trouble so we don't have to rely completely on Christ. To have true humility we must surrender everything to him. He gave his life for you. Give everything to him. Why try to shoulder a burden when it isn't necessary? Jesus wants to share his strength and grace with you. Don't resist but give everything to him. The Bible tells us that worrying does nothing for us. It doesn't make things happen faster. Usually it might seem to take forever. It can rob us of sleep, joy, and add stress to our lives.

I have spent so much wasted time in my life worrying about things I know I had absolutely no control over. It can be difficult to let things go because it makes us feel helpless and weak. That is simply not true. If you are holding onto something and ruminate about it over and over again causing sleepless nights and tired days, lay it at the feet of Christ and let him take it for you. He is waiting for you.

Things I Am Anxious or Worried about Today:

_____

_____

_____

_____

_____

_____

_____

_____

_____

_____

_____

_____

_____

Today's Prayer

Dear Jesus, I give all the things I have listed here over to you. I confess I am worried and anxious about what will happen. Help me to release them into your care and help me to trust in you. Amen.

> The LORD is my shepherd; I shall not want. He maketh me to lie down in green pastures: he leadeth me beside the still waters. He restoreth my soul: he leadeth me in the paths of righteousness for his name's sake. (Psalm 23:1–3 KJV)

DAY 18

The Peace of God

> Be careful for nothing; but in every thing by prayer and supplication with thanksgiving let your requests be made known unto God. And the peace of God, which passeth all understanding, shall keep your hearts and minds through Christ Jesus. (Philippians 4:6–7 KJV)

In this passage we see a three-step process for dealing with life. First is prayer. Prayer is a two-way conversation between God and his child. We talk to God then we need to wait for him to talk to us instead of rattling off a list of requests and needs and then getting up and leaving. Second is supplications which are the requests and concerns we have, asking for God's guidance and wisdom.

Last is thanksgiving. Giving thanks to God for all the blessings in your life. Do you have food? Shelter? A job? When did you last thank God for those things? We are told what the result will be when we do this. God's peace will keep, or watch over and sustain, both your heart and mind. Peace is something sought after by so many. We have a direct line to the prince of peace, Jesus. Use it but do not abuse it. Do not be like the Pharisees but go into your quiet place and talk with your Savior. Have a time of quiet meditation free of distraction. Another favorite song of mine is "In the Garden" by C. Austin Miles, 1913. Here is the first verse and refrain:

I come to the garden alone,
While the dew is still on the roses;

And the voice I hear, falling on my ear,
The Son of God discloses.

And He walks with me, and He talks with me,
And He tells me I am His own,
And the joy we share as we tarry there,
None other has ever known.

Thoughts and Notes:

_____

_____

_____

_____

_____

_____

_____

_____

_____

_____

_____

Today's Prayer:

Dear Jesus, help me to be silent and listen for your voice and not just make countless requests. Help me to treat our time together with the sincerity and honesty it demands. I thank you for everything, big and small, that you do for me each and every day. Let me know the peace that is beyond my understanding. In your name. Amen.

LET NOT YOUR HEART BE TROUBLED

Peace I leave with you, my peace I give unto you: not as the world giveth, give I unto you. Let not your heart be troubled, neither let it be afraid. (John 14:27 KJV)

Little Is Much

In Jesus's miracle in the feeding of the multitude, there is much we can learn. There were five thousand men and an unknown number of women and children. The disciples, like us so many times, were not focusing on the right thing. They wanted to send the people away so they can provide for themselves. When Jesus told them to feed them, they didn't believe they could. They were focused on the material. They had the Son of God in their midst but didn't recognize what that meant in that moment. Jesus took what to some seemed so insignificant in light of the task, blessed it, and it didn't just satisfy the need but went well above and beyond the need with twelve baskets of leftovers, not just a few crumbs.

Do you sell yourself short thinking your talents and abilities are not sufficient to do something for God? A small boy with a small sacrifice was used mightily by Jesus to abundantly satisfy the need of thousands. Just think what he can do with you when you step out in faith and believe. Jesus can solve any problem. We just need to trust and obey. Jesus specializes in taking the small or weak of the world and doing incredible things.

Thoughts and Notes:

_____

_____

_____

_____

_____

_____

_____

_____

_____

_____

_____

_____

_____

Today's Prayer

Dear Jesus, please help me to never think that something or someone is too insignificant to be mightily used by you for great things. Let me pray believing and expecting that my, or anyone else's gifts, are worth bringing to you. You can work a miracle with anything brought to you. Thank you for loving me and caring for me. Amen.

DAY 20

Humble Pie

> Let this mind be in you, which was also in Christ Jesus: Who, being in the form of God, thought it not robbery to be equal with God: But made himself of no reputation, and took upon him the form of a servant, and was made in the likeness of men: And being found in fashion as a man, he humbled himself, and became obedient unto death, even the death of the cross. (Philippians 2:5–8 KJV)

Jesus's fellowship and communion with God is something beyond what we can understand. Before Jesus became a human man he had never experienced the weakness we do. He never had experienced being tired or feeling pain. Jesus was a carpenter. Do you think he ever hit his finger with a hammer and felt that all-too-human temptation to say something naughty? Okay, perhaps I digress a bit. Leaving the paradise of heaven and putting himself into a weak human vessel to go through every temptation and problems we would face in our lives is in itself the greatest humility.

But Jesus went far beyond just that. He let himself be killed, not just any death, but probably the most excruciating and horrible death anyone could go through. I remember watching the *Passion of the Christ* the first time. While it gave a glimpse of what the process of crucifixion encompassed, which was truly heart-wrenching, it was just scratching the surface. Roman soldiers knew exactly how to make it as painful as possible. It was hours and hours on incomprehensible pain and suffering that Jesus endured for his people. And if that wasn't enough, the wrath of God, his Father, was poured out in full upon him for all the sins of his children. We couldn't bear the tiniest portion of God's wrath, but Jesus took it all.

How often do we thank our Lord for what he did and endured for us? Our trials and tribulations we face are incomparable. We need to be reminded what Jesus did for us and let it humble us. Let it also encourage us to be more like Christ and know that he went through all this because he loved us. And if he loved us that much, he will never be anywhere except right beside us our whole life.

Thoughts and Notes:

_____

_____

_____

_____

_____

_____

_____

_____

_____

_____

_____

_____

_____

_____

Today's Prayer

Dear Jesus, I can never offer enough thanks for what you suffered for me. My mind and heart are humbled and broken trying to fathom it. Please never let me take for granted your sacrifice and let me be constantly thankful for the sacrifice you made. Amen.

DAY 21

Today do two things: First take a part of your day and make a list of all the things you are thankful for. Then go to God in prayer and thank him for each and every one.

Then go to a loved one and tell them how thankful you are to have them in your life and thankful for the things they do for you. Call a friend you perhaps haven't spoken to for a while and tell them thank you. Encouraging others has a benefit of being encouraged yourself. We are commanded in scripture to life each other up. Do so and see what happens.

Day 22

Call to the Lost

One of the most frequently asked questions that unbelievers pose is the existence of evil and the existence of a loving God. It seems to them, perhaps, that the two should not exist at that same time. There are many forms of evil. Moral, natural, intellectual, emotional, etc. and the root cause of all of them is sin. Humankind is responsible for sin in all of the mentioned forms. Sin affected not just mankind but all of creation. Before man's sin there was no evil present in creation. Christians also have asked questions about this topic. God provided the solution for this by sacrificing his son. He did not have to do that. He could have just washed his hand of humanity entirely but instead gave us a way back to him.

I didn't, at the time and for many years after, understand why God allowed cancer to take my father when I was fifteen. As I grew up and went through so many rough periods, I would miss him very much and I know my siblings have felt the same way at times. But I would not be here now doing what I am doing and be where I am had my father not died then. I met my best friend, and despite my bumbling and mistakes, God used me to lead him to Christ. My point in all of this is that God is indeed loving and good despite our lack of understanding.

I came across a very good quote from Dorothy Sayers as I was doing a bit a research: "For whatever reason God chose to make man as he is—limited and suffering and subject to sorrows and death— He had the honesty and the courage to take His own medicine. Whatever game he is playing with His creation, He has kept his own rules and played fair. He can exact nothing from man that He has not exacted from Himself. He has Himself gone through the whole of human experience, from the trivial irritations of family life and the cramping restrictions of hard work and lack of money to the worst horrors of pain and humiliation, defeat, despair, and death. When He was a man, He played the man. He was born in poverty and died in disgrace and thought it well worthwhile."[2]

So for you who may be questioning whether you should follow God and accept Jesus into your heart to be your Lord, your friend, your helper…ask yourself what would happen to you should you die tomorrow? Jesus died a horrible death for you. Put aside your doubts and take a step in faith and you will not once regret it. Pray a simple prayer something like this:

Dear Jesus, I confess that I have sinned and I need you to be my Savior. I believe you died on the cross and paid the price for my sin. I believe you rose again just as you said you would and will one day come and take me home to be in heaven with you forever. Please come into my life and be my Lord.

> Softly and tenderly Jesus is calling,
> calling for you and for me;
> see, on the portals he's waiting and watching,
> watching for you and for me.
>
> Come home, come home;
> you who are weary come home;
> earnestly, tenderly, Jesus is calling,
> calling, O sinner, come home!

"Softly and Tenderly" (Will Thompson, 1880)

[2.] Dorothy Sayers, *Creed or Chaos?*

Are You Sure about This, God?

Doubt is something, that at some point in a Christian's life, that has to be dealt with. It can be doubt about what his will is or if God will answer our prayer or doubt about an answer to our prayer. Doubt is not something to be ashamed of. God is very much aware that we simply get scared or impatient or confused about things that happen in our lives and that it causes us to doubt him. Scripture abounds with great men of the faith who experienced doubt. Usually the first to come to mind is Thomas. You would think that one who had been so close to Jesus would not doubt. In the end Jesus did not chastise Thomas but stood before him and told him: "Reach hither thy finger, and behold my hands; and reach hither thy hand, and thrust it into my side: and be not faithless, but believing" (John 20:27 KJV). Thomas didn't do that though. He acknowledged Jesus as Lord and God.

Doubt can sabotage our walk with Christ in many ways. It can limit our prayers to small simple things. Unchecked doubt is probably the most devastating thing a Christian can have. We must constantly remind ourselves of who our God is and that there is absolutely nothing beyond God's power and no one who cannot be changed. No situation is beyond his ability to fix. As I have pointed out in other posts God's timing is not ours. A prayer that doesn't immediately get an answer does not mean it will not ever be answered. Keep this firmly established in the front of your mind and trust him.

Proverbs 3:5–8 (KJV) tells us to "trust in the LORD with all thine heart; and lean not unto thine own understanding. In all thy ways acknowledge him, and he shall direct thy paths. Be not wise in thine own eyes: fear the LORD, and depart from evil. It shall be health to thy navel, and marrow to thy bones." We must trust with *all* our heart, not just some of it. Acknowledge him in *all* our ways, not just some of them.

Thoughts and Notes:

_____

_____

_____

_____

_____

_____

_____

_____

_____

_____

_____

_____

Today's Prayer

Heavenly Father, I have trouble sometimes believing in your will and plan for my life. Forgive me for doubting and not trusting you completely. Help me understand that you do not punish me when I doubt and that you understand my weaknesses. Help me reject all thoughts of doubt when they arise and help me trust you completely. In your precious name. Amen.

But my God shall supply all your need
according to his riches in glory by Christ Jesus.
(Philippians 4:19 KJV)

DAY 24

Miracles

Have you ever had a front-row seat to a miracle? Miracles are all around us, although not necessarily the raising the dead or parting the sea type. An unbeliever coming to Christ, healing from a disease or narrowly surviving an accident, are just a few examples. I would like to share one that occurred when I was sixteen.

In that summer of 1988 I toured with an evangelistic music organization called the Continental Singers and Orchestra. At that time there were several dozen groups that went all over the world spreading the gospel through song and film. My group, Tour I, crisscrossed the United States but also spent a week in Bangalore and Mumbai (formerly known as Bombay), India, showing the Jesus film. That time of the year in India was in the middle of the monsoon season where it would sometimes dump buckets of rain without any or little notice.

One evening while we were preparing to perform our final number, our sponsor informed us we had to stop because you could just feel it in the air that we were about to get swamped. So instead of packing everything up and hitting the road, we all gathered into a group and prayed for weather to hold so we could finish our concert. I will never forget looking up just before we started and saw a huge patch of crystal-clear sky with the moon and stars shining brightly. Everywhere else you could look was nothing but clouds. That clear patch of sky was not there moments before. Our sponsors were rather amazed, and so was I. Well as we finished our last number we felt the first few drops of rain start. We hustled like crazy and packed up our sensitive electronic equipment before it really hit. God stepped in and let us finish.

Ever so often you see a movie about something terrible that happens that modern technology or medicine say is impossible to recover from or impossible to solve. Rubbish, I tell you. God holds the very fabric of the entire universe perfectly in exactly the right measurements. If God can do that, do you really think he can't solve any problem we may have? The question is, do you ask for the miracles or just ask for the small things? Maybe we don't experience the big miracles because we do not ask and pray for them and continue praying for them until they happen.

Thoughts and Notes:

_____
_____
_____
_____
_____
_____
_____
_____
_____
_____
_____
_____
_____
_____

Today's Prayer

Jesus, miracle worker, please help me to not be afraid to ask for miracles in my life and those close to me and in the world around me. Help me come boldly before your throne expecting miracles and believing you are powerful enough to do anything. Amen.

Behold, I am the LORD, the God of all flesh: *is there any thing too hard for me?* (Jeremiah 32:27 KJV)

The Master's Touch

An old song came to mind today that was taken from on old poem by Myra Brooks Welch in 1921. It paints a vivid picture that can apply to both Christians who may think they've lost their way and have nothing of use to offer God. And to the unbeliever who has suffered mistreatment and abuse from the world but can find purpose in the Master's hands.

'Twas battered and scarred, and the auctioneer thought it scarcely worth his while to waste much time on the old violin, but held it up with a smile.

"What am I bidden, good folks," he cried.

"Who'll start the bidding for me?"

"A dollar, a dollar. Then two! Only two? Two dollars, and who'll make it three?"

"Three dollars, once; three dollars, twice; going for three…"

But no, from the room, far back, a gray-haired man came forward and picked up the bow; Then wiping the dust from the old violin, and tightening the loose strings, he played a melody pure and sweet, as a caroling angel sings.

The music ceased, and the auctioneer, with a voice that was quiet and low, said: "What am I bid for the old violin?"

And he held it up with the bow.

"A thousand dollars, and who'll make it two? Two thousand! And who'll make it three? Three thousand, once; three thousand, twice, and going and gone," said he.

The people cheered, but some of them cried, "We do not quite understand. What changed its worth?" Swift came the reply: "The touch of a Master's hand."

And many a man with life out of tune, and battered and scarred with sin, Is auctioned cheap to the thoughtless crowd much like the old violin.

A "mess of pottage," a glass of wine, a game—and he travels on.

"He is going" once, and "going" twice, He's "going" and almost "gone."

But the Master comes, and the foolish crowd never can quite understand the worth of a soul and the change that's wrought by the touch of the Master's hand.

> Come home, lost one. Leave the world
> behind and surrender to the Master's hand.

Today's Prayer

Father, I thank you for taking what the world casts aside and deems it no value and making something priceless and beautiful. Help me to point others to you and tell them of how much better their lives will become if they let themselves be touched by the Master's hand. Amen.

Forgive

I'm sure we have all heard the old adage "forgive and forget." But honestly how well do any of us do that? Our human nature wants to pay that person back for a wrongdoing done to us. The disease of unforgiveness. Yes, it is a disease that will cripple our fellowship with God and with others. Unforgiveness, like a disease, will permeate and sink its tendrils into every part of our lives. It can affect our health, increase stress, affect work, appetite, and relationships with everyone. It destroys your joy.

Forgiveness is something you do for yourself. However wrong something was that was done to you, and it definitely could be, holding onto a grudge does nothing beneficial to you. It is a self-perpetuating destructive thing that we must overcome to live a godly life.

The good news is that you do not have to do it alone. Jesus knows the difficulties we have in letting go of those feelings of revenge, resentment, and anger we experience. If we ask him to help us get past those negative things, he will. Seek out your pastor or another close friend to pray with you. It will not necessarily happen overnight, and it may be one of the more difficult things you ever do. But it is far, far better to do it than not.

Thoughts and Notes:

_____
_____
_____
_____
_____
_____
_____
_____
_____
_____
_____
_____

Today's Prayer

Heavenly Father, please help me forgive. Let me see how much it harms me physically, mentally, emotionally, and how much it prohibits me from having joy and peace with you and others. I confess I cannot do this on my own. I need you to come along beside me and help me let go of all the feelings of vengeance and bitterness I may have. Amen.

> Put on therefore, as the elect of God, holy and beloved, bowels of mercies, kindness, humbleness of mind, meekness, longsuffering; Forbearing one another, and forgiving one another, if any man have a quarrel against any: even as Christ forgave you, so also do ye. (Colossians 3:12–13 KJV)

The Refuge

He that dwelleth in the secret place of the most High shall abide under the shadow of the Almighty. I will say of the Lord, He is my refuge and my fortress: my God; in him will I trust. Surely he shall deliver thee from the snare of the fowler, and from the noisome pestilence. He shall cover thee with his feathers, and under his wings shalt thou trust: his truth shall be thy shield and buckler.

Thou shalt not be afraid for the terror by night; nor for the arrow that flieth by day; Nor for the pestilence that walketh in darkness; nor for the destruction that wasteth at noonday. A thousand shall fall at thy side, and ten thousand at thy right hand; but it shall not come nigh thee. Only with thine eyes shalt thou behold and see the reward of the wicked. Because thou hast made the Lord, which is my refuge, even the most High, thy habitation; There shall no evil befall thee, neither shall any plague come nigh thy dwelling. (Psalm 91:1–10 KJV)

This part of Psalm 91 is full of wonderful promises. But it does require some effort on our part. We must go and dwell in the secret place. We must go into the fortress to receive the benefits of it.

This psalm is the antidote for when we are feeling afraid, overwhelmed, and anxious. I am guilty of sometimes trying to tackle a problem or face my fears without God and it never has ended well. The problem becomes bigger and harder to solve afterward. When we act alone to face our problems, they can easily defeat us. Pray this Psalm over and over and say it aloud not just silently in your mind. Keep repeating it and claim the promises made to us. God is faithful. Trust him.

Thoughts and Notes:

_____

_____

_____

_____

_____

_____

_____

_____

_____

_____

_____

_____

_____

_____

Today's Prayer

Jesus, I thank you that despite whatever happens, I have a place to run to and be safe and secure. Help me to learn not to be afraid of anything and help me to dwell in the secret place and abide. Amen.

"A mighty fortress is our God, a bulwark never failing!"

From "A Mighty Fortress Is Our God" (Martin Luther, 1529)

Step into the Light

Who are you? I don't mean your name or who your family is or what your occupation is. Who are you when no one else is around? Would you be someone that you would be ashamed of if you were that person out in public? Sometimes we get caught up in a particular habit and lifestyle that we would be ashamed of if it became known. It could become an addiction if unchecked, or perhaps it already is for you. Addiction is a form of slavery. Slavery to something or someone.

One effective way to prevent this is to be consistent in God's Word every day and with God's people every chance you get. Whatever we feed in our lives through actions, thoughts, or words, good or bad, is what will grow in us. The light of God's Word, as sharp as a two-edged sword, has the power to conquer anything. Sometimes you may need help from a pastor or godly counselor. Letting whatever destructive habit come into the light of God's Word, allowing friends and family to pray over you and with you, and most importantly spending time alone with God to gain strength and grace, will be the cure.

Establish consistency in all these areas. Use a journal to write down your thoughts and concerns and use it when you pray. Do not lose heart if you don't succeed right away. Step into the light and let God begin to help you.

Thoughts and Notes:

_____
_____
_____
_____
_____
_____
_____
_____
_____
_____
_____
_____
_____
_____

Today's Prayer

Jesus, help me to examine my life and if there are any habits or addictions that are causing me to stumble and behave in any way that isn't honoring to you, give me the courage to use every tool and resource to get rid of them. Forgive me when I fail at this. In your name, Amen.

There hath no temptation taken you but such as is common to man: but God is faithful, who will not suffer you to be tempted above that ye are able; but will with the temptation also make a way to escape, that ye may be able to bear it. (1 Corinthians 10:13 KJV)

When God Doesn't Make Sense

My best friend and I meet at least once a week for lunch and conversation. Topics range from movies to deep theological discussions. A couple months ago I was laid off from my job for the second time from the same place. This last time was after ten years. My friend still works there and did before my time in the same department. During one conversation about our employer I found out that in 2018, before I had my first shoulder injury at work, our supervisor had mentioned to my friend and another coworker in our department that perhaps my position should be eliminated.

Well in November of 2018 I fell at work and tore up my shoulder pretty bad. A few months of therapy followed by not one, but two surgeries about a year apart took me into March of 2021 when after a final visit to the surgeon my status was designated fully recovered. Two months after that my position was eliminated.

In 2018 I was not in nearly as good of a place, especially financially, as I am now, although I still have a lot of debt. The point I want to make is that there was a purpose God had for me injuring my shoulder and taking it so long to finally recover. During those two years, two surgeries, and months in between of tough physical therapy, my employer couldn't really lay me off and I was able to keep my job and benefits and in the end got a nice settlement from workman's comp. Sure I could have thought of some better and less painful ways for God to perhaps work his purpose. But here on the other side of all of what happened, I see clearly why it happened. I may not have ever begun my blog and started trying to find ways to support myself outside the normal workforce had I not been laid off. God's purpose for our lives will not always be pleasant, but I can attest that it always become clear to us in time and always is for our benefit.

Thoughts and Notes:

_____

_____

_____

_____

_____

_____

_____

_____

_____

_____

_____

_____

Today's Prayer

Heavenly Father, I do not always understand why sometimes it is necessary for me to go through pain and trials to fulfill your purpose for me. Give me overwhelming strength and grace and, most importantly, help me to trust that you are working in whatever happens in my life for my benefit. Amen.

Day 30

God Is Not Done

On the last day of this journey I thought I'd briefly share a few statistics. It may seem, if you listen to much of the news, that evil is getting stronger and the world is falling away from God very fast. This could be true in some parts of the world. But in other countries, Christianity is taking the world by storm.

According to Wikipedia, "Christianity has been estimated to be growing rapidly in South America, Africa, and Asia. In Africa, for instance, in 1900, there were only 8.7 million adherents of Christianity; now there are 390 million (382,000 per year), and it is expected that by 2025 there will be 600 million Christians in Africa."

According to the World Christian Encyclopedia, "Approximately 2.7 million people convert to Christianity annually from another religion, with Christianity ranking first in net gains through religious conversion." That is just shy of 7,400 per day!

This is truly amazing. God's Word is not weak and the gospel is stronger than ever. Do not let yourself get discouraged by what you may hear around you. Remember…

This is my Father's world, and to my listening ears
All nature sings, and round me rings the music of the spheres.
This is my Father's world: I rest me in the thought
Of rocks and trees, of skies and seas;
His hand the wonders wrought.

This is my Father's world, the birds their carols raise,
The morning light, the lily white, declare their Maker's praise.
This is my Father's world: He shines in all that's fair;
In the rustling grass I hear Him pass;
He speaks to me everywhere.

This is my Father's world. O let me ne'er forget
That though the wrong seems oft so strong, God is the ruler yet.
This is my Father's world: the battle is not done:
Jesus Who died shall be satisfied,
And earth and Heav'n be one.

This is my Father's world, dreaming, I see His face.
I open my eyes, and in glad surprise cry, "The Lord is in this place."
This is my Father's world, from the shining courts above,
The Beloved One, His Only Son,
Came—a pledge of deathless love.

This is my Father's world, should my heart be ever sad?
The lord is King—let the heavens ring.
God reigns—let the earth be glad.
This is my Father's world. Now closer to Heaven bound,
For dear to God is the earth Christ trod.
No place but is holy ground.

This is my Father's world. I walk a desert lone.
In a bush ablaze to my wondering gaze
God makes His glory known.
This is my Father's world, a wanderer I may roam
Whate'er my lot, it matters not,
My heart is still at home.

"This Is My Father's World" (Maltbie D. Babcock, 1901)

References

Fanny Crosby. *America's Hymn Queen*. http://www.christianhistory-timeline.com/GLIMPSEF/Glimpses2/glimpses198.shtml.
Dorothy Sayers. *Creed or Chaos?* New York, Harcourt Brace, 1949, p. 4.

About the Author

Born and raised in Alaska, Jason Curry came to know Christ as his savior at the age of nine at an Awana function. In his youth and early adulthood, he had the privilege of traveling all over the world with his musical abilities. He spent a dozen years in East Texas in various retail and management jobs before returning to his home in Alaska.

Jason is an avid reader and movie buff. He is the youngest of five children and has a rich background in music. In his nearly forty-one years as a child of God, he has had a front-row seat to some wonderful and heartbreaking things. But he is still going strong thanks to his Lord and Savior Jesus.

Printed in the USA
CPSIA information can be obtained
at www.ICGtesting.com
LVHW071950170923
758232LV00084B/822